# The Melodies That Misled

## Debunking the Mozart Effect

Freudian Trips

# Copyright Page

# Disclaimer

The views and opinions expressed in this book are those of the author(s) and do not necessarily reflect the official policy or position of any other agency, organization, employer, or company. The contents of this book are for informational and educational purposes only and are not intended to serve as professional advice, diagnosis, or treatment.

The information provided in this book is believed to be accurate and reliable as of the date of publication. However, it may include some errors or inaccuracies, and no warranty or guarantee is provided regarding the accuracy, timeliness, or applicability of the content.

Readers are encouraged to consult with professional philosophers, educators, or other qualified professionals where appropriate for personalized advice. The author(s) and publisher shall not be liable for any loss, damage, or harm caused or alleged to be caused, directly or indirectly, by the information or ideas contained, suggested, or referenced in this book.

By reading this book, the reader acknowledges and agrees that they are solely responsible for how they interpret and apply the information contained herein.

This book may also include references to other works, studies, and sources. These references are provided for further reading and exploration and do not imply endorsement or validation of the specific theories, viewpoints, or interpretations presented in those works.

# Introduction: The Music That Promised Miracles

Imagine if simply pressing play on a CD could instantly boost your brainpower. Well, that's exactly what the world started to believe back in 1993. It all started with a scientific study that seemed to suggest that listening to a bit of music by the famous composer Mozart could make you temporarily smarter.

This idea, which quickly became known as the "Mozart Effect," sent shockwaves through the world. Suddenly, parents were playing Mozart to their babies, students were blasting it before exams, and businesses even pumped his melodies into their offices. Everyone wanted a piece of this musical miracle.

The Mozart Effect wasn't claiming that music could make you a genius overnight. The idea was that it specifically tuned up a part of your brain responsible for things like visualizing shapes or mentally navigating a maze. It was like a quick workout for a specific mental muscle.

Of course, music has always held a special power over us. It can make us laugh, cry, dance, or feel incredibly relaxed. Science has even shown that music can help with things like pain relief and memory. But the Mozart Effect felt different – as if scientists had suddenly unlocked a secret code within the melodies. Was it all too good to be true? Let's dive in and find out!

# Chapter 1: The Science Behind the Hype

Remember that promise of music making you smarter? Well, it all started with a pretty small experiment. In 1993, three scientists decided to see if listening to music could affect how well college students did on a specific type of brain puzzle.

**The Setup**

They gathered 36 students and split them into three groups. Here's what each group experienced:

- **Group 1: The Mozart Crew** - These students got to relax for ten minutes while listening to a piece of music by Mozart.
- **Group 2: The Chill-Out Squad** - This group also got to relax for ten minutes but listened to spoken relaxation instructions instead of music.
- **Group 3: The Silent Bunch** - These folks got ten minutes of plain old silence.

### The Brain Challenge

After their listening (or not listening) session, all the students had to tackle the same puzzle. This puzzle was all about folding and cutting paper in your mind and imagining what shape it would make when unfolded. Think of it as a mental origami challenge.

### The "Eureka!" Moment

The scientists discovered that the Mozart group did slightly better on the puzzle than the other two groups. It wasn't a huge difference, but it was enough to make them say, "Hmmm, there might be something going on here!"

The media went wild over this. Headlines started popping up about how Mozart could make you smarter. But it's important to remember that this was just one study, with a small group of people, focused on a very specific kind of thinking.

### How Did This Study Stand Out?

Most research on music and the brain had looked at things like how music affects mood or helps with memory. This study was different because it seemed to suggest that music could directly improve your ability to solve a totally unrelated mental task, even if it was just for a short while.

# Chapter 2: When Science Meets Marketing

The results of that little college experiment didn't stay quietly tucked away in a science journal. Instead, news of the "Mozart Effect" spread like wildfire. Newspapers, magazines, and TV shows couldn't get enough of this story. It was the perfect combination – a catchy idea about music, brains, and a sprinkle of genius from a world-famous composer.

Suddenly, everyone wanted in on the Mozart magic. Companies raced to create products promising to boost your baby's brainpower:

- **Mozart CDs for Babies:** Shelves filled up with CDs promising to turn your little one into a mini-Einstein, all thanks to the power of classical music.
- **Mozart for Expecting Moms** – The idea was to expose the baby to Mozart's music even before birth, giving them a headstart on intelligence.

- **Mozart Toys and Books:** Colorful toys playing Mozart tunes and books claiming to "boost your child's IQ" popped up in stores.

It wasn't just about babies and kids. Businesses jumped on the bandwagon too:

- **Mozart in the Office:** Companies piped classical music into their offices, hoping that the melodies would make their workers smarter and more productive.
- **Mozart for Studying:** Students were encouraged to blast Mozart in their headphones while hitting the books, hoping for a little extra brain boost.

**The Media Machine**

The media played a huge role in making the Mozart Effect a sensation. Headlines didn't focus on the limited scope of the original study, instead, they blared out messages like "Mozart Makes You Smarter!" and "Boost Your Baby's Brain With Music!"

It was a classic case of exciting scientific findings getting oversimplified and blown out of proportion. The idea of a quick and easy way to get smarter was just too tempting to resist.

But as we'll see in the next chapters, when the excitement settled down, and scientists started taking a closer look, the Mozart Effect started to lose its melody.

# Chapter 3: The Music Fades - When Science Hits Repeat

You might think that once scientists discover something amazing, it's set in stone. But that's not quite how science works. One of the most important things a scientist does is try to repeat an experiment to see if they get the same results again. We call this "replication."

**Why "Do It Again" Matters**

Think of it like baking a new recipe. The first time might turn out delicious, but what if it was just a fluke? Maybe the oven was hotter than usual, or you accidentally used a bit too much sugar. Baking it again is the only way to know if the recipe truly works.

Science is the same way. One study might show something exciting, but it could be a fluke. Repeating the study with different people, in different settings, is what helps us figure out if the original finding was real and reliable.

**The Mozart Effect Strikes a Sour Note**

Many scientists were intrigued (and some were skeptical) about the Mozart Effect. So, labs all over the world started running their versions of the original experiment. Some closely followed the original setup, others made slight changes. But the results were all over the place:

- **Mixed Bag:** Some studies did show a small, short-term boost for the Mozart listeners, but it wasn't always consistent.
- **No Boost At All:** Many other studies found absolutely no difference in puzzle performance between those who listened to Mozart, other kinds of music, or just sat in silence.
- **Enjoyment Factor:** Interestingly, some researchers started to notice that any enjoyable activity, whether it was listening to a favorite pop song or reading a funny story, could give the same short-term mental boost.

## The Puzzle of Inconsistency

Scientists began to analyze why they weren't getting the same clear-cut "Mozart Effect" result. They considered factors like the choice of music, the length of time people listened, and even the types of puzzles and mental tasks people were given. The picture got more and more muddled.

Sadly for Mozart, it was starting to look like his music didn't hold that magical brain-boosting power the headlines had promised.

# Chapter 4: The Myth Unravels

As more and more studies were done, scientists began to shift their views. The initial excitement about the Mozart Effect started to fade. It wasn't that music suddenly lost its power, but the idea that Mozart's music specifically held a secret key to unlocking our intelligence just didn't hold up under closer examination.

Why did the Mozart Effect Crumble? Here's what scientists pointed out:

- **Small Start:** The original study had a very small number of participants. Small studies can be useful for finding *possible* effects, but they aren't strong enough to prove something works for everybody.
- **Short and Sweet...Too Sweet?** The mental boost seen in the original study was very short-lived. It was like a quick sugar rush for the brain, not a long-term improvement plan.

- **What About the LONG Game?** No studies managed to show that listening to Mozart led to lasting changes in intelligence or any meaningful skills.

## One Study Doesn't Tell the Whole Story

The Mozart Effect is a powerful reminder that a single, exciting study is just the beginning of scientific discovery, not the end. It's like seeing a single interesting snapshot – it might hint at something bigger, but you need the whole photo album to see the complete picture.

Science builds on itself. One study leads to more questions, more experiments, and a more refined understanding of how things work. In the case of the Mozart Effect, the more scientists looked, the less evidence they found for that initial "wow" result.

While the idea of a musical shortcut to a super-brain may have faded, that doesn't mean the story ends there. Let's explore why music still holds incredible power for our minds, just maybe not the kind of power we initially hoped for.

# Chapter 5: Melodies That Matter

While Mozart's music might not turn you into an instant genius, that doesn't mean we should throw those CDs out the window! Music has a remarkable way of touching our lives, even if it doesn't magically reshape our brains overnight.

**Music, the Stress Buster:** Ever put on your favorite song and felt a wave of calm wash over you? Music has a real knack for lowering levels of stress hormones in our bodies. It's like a soundtrack for relaxation, helping us unwind after a tough day.

**The Mood Maestro:** Music is a master at playing with our emotions. A bouncy, upbeat tune can put a pep in our step, a sad song can help us cry it out, and a powerful piece of music can send shivers down our spines. Music speaks directly to our hearts.

**Memory Lane Stroll** Studies have shown that music can be a powerful memory trigger, especially for people living with conditions like dementia. A familiar song from the past can reconnect them with moments and emotions, even when other memories fade.

**Creativity Spark:** Ever find yourself humming along to a song and suddenly bursting with new ideas? Music can act like a creativity jumpstart. It gets our brains buzzing and can help us think outside the box.

## Music is More Than Mozart

The Mozart Effect may have captured hearts (and wallets) for a while, but the truth is that the power of music doesn't rest on a single composer, Instead, it's about the personal connection we feel with music:

- The songs that get us dancing.
- The melodies that bring back cherished memories.
- The pieces of music that take our breath away with their beauty.

Music has always been part of what makes us human. It's a way to express ourselves, connect with others, and find joy, comfort, and inspiration. And that's something no scientific study can take away.

# Chapter 6: Beyond the Music – When Science Gets Misunderstood

The rise and fall of the Mozart Effect teaches us something important that goes far beyond music. It's a reminder of how easily exciting but incomplete science can be twisted into promises of quick fixes and miracle cures, especially when it comes to things as complex as the human brain.

## Our Wish For Easy Answers

Let's be honest, we all want solutions that are quick, easy, and guaranteed to work. Think about all the fad diets, get-rich-quick schemes, and "life hacks" that become popular. Our brains are wired to seek shortcuts, and that desire spills over into how we understand science, too.

The Mozart Effect seemed like the perfect answer. Pop in a CD, and voila – smarter! The truth is, improving our minds, our health, or our lives usually requires more effort and doesn't come with easy one-size-fits-all formulas.

## When Science Hype Meets the Media

The media, with its need for catchy headlines and simple stories, can sometimes play a role in spreading exaggerated or misleading interpretations of science. That little experiment about Mozart and brain puzzles snowballed into a global phenomenon because it was an irresistible story promising amazing results.

## Responsibility Check

Both scientists and the media have a responsibility to communicate science clearly and responsibly.

- **Scientists:** They need to be clear about the limitations of their studies and avoid making grand promises based on early, limited findings.
- **Media:** They need to report scientific discoveries responsibly, making it clear if a finding is preliminary, done with small groups, or needs much more research to be truly understood.

## Staying Savvy

The Mozart Effect is a reminder to be skeptical not just about music but about all the "miracle cures" and sensational science claims that bombard us daily. Ask questions like:

- Does this sound too good to be true?
- Is it based on one small study or a solid body of research?
- Are they trying to sell me something based on this science?

Science is an amazing tool for understanding the world, but it's important to remember that it's a process, not a magic wand. Let's celebrate the real power of music, develop healthy skepticism about flashy claims, and champion the search for real, evidence-based knowledge!

# Conclusion: Finding the Right Rhythm

Our journey through the story of the Mozart Effect has taken us from excitement to skepticism and finally to a clearer perspective on both the power and the limits of music's influence on our minds. So, where do we land?

**Key Takeaways:**

- **Music is powerful...but not magic:** Music can move us deeply, reduce stress, spark memories, and provide pure joy, but it's not a shortcut to a supercharged brain.
- **The lure of the easy answer:** We need to be wary of sensational claims and "miracle cures" – especially when it comes to something as complex as the human brain.
- **Science is a journey:** Exciting discoveries take time to verify. One study isn't the whole story, and responsible science reporting is key to avoiding hype.

The Mozart Effect might not have lived up to its initial promise, but that doesn't mean the story ends there. Scientists continue to explore the intricate relationship between music and our brains:

- **Music for healing:** Research is exploring the potential for music to help people with brain injuries, Parkinson's disease, or mood disorders.
- **Music and development:** We might learn even more about how music supports healthy development in children, impacting language, creativity, and more.
- **The joy factor:** Ultimately, the greatest power of music might lie in its ability to connect us, make us feel, and bring pure enjoyment to our lives.

While we might have to retire the idea of Mozart turning us into instant geniuses, the melody of science continues to play on. One day, we may uncover even deeper ways music shapes our minds and enriches our lives. For now, we can enjoy the music we love and remember – its true power might be greater than we ever first imagined.

# About Freudian Trips

Welcome to Freudian Trips, your dedicated platform for diving deep into the world of psychology. We are more than just a YouTube channel or a book publisher. We are a beacon of enlightenment, making complex psychological concepts accessible and engaging for all.

Our YouTube channel is a rich repository of psychology made simple. We take the profound and often complex ideas from the world of psychology and break them down into digestible, easy-to-understand content. From the foundational theories of Freud to the cognitive insights of Piaget, we cover a broad spectrum of psychological schools and thoughts, making psychology accessible to everyone, regardless of their background or prior knowledge.

As a book publisher, we take the same approach, transforming intricate psychological theories into comprehensible narratives. Our books are not just collections of words, but vessels of wisdom that make psychology approachable and relatable. We believe that psychology should not be confined to academic circles, but should be available to all who seek to understand the human mind and behavior.

At Freudian Trips, we believe in the power of curiosity and the pursuit of knowledge. We are here to stoke the fires of your curiosity, to guide you on your intellectual journey, and to help you navigate the fascinating world of psychology.

If you are someone who is not afraid to question, to explore, and to learn, then you are in the right place. Join us on this journey of exploration, as we make psychology easy to understand, one concept at a time.

Be sure to visit our Youtube channel at:
www.freudiantrips.com/youtube

You can also visit us on the web at www.freudiantrips.com

Welcome to The Freudian Trip community. Stay curious. Stay enlightened.

# The
# BORAX
# BOOK

## Incredible Uses for Borax


*N.D. Lorenz*

Welcome to the Borax Book. From the writer of <u>Borax Girl</u> comes the research of the incredible uses of the product Borax - a quick guide to this amazing product. Banned by pharmaceutical giants in other countries when they discovered how great it really is and could not be patented, we are grateful to still have this "laundry booster" available to us, and at such a reasonable price, on our store shelves in America.

# Contents

# Borax for Health

Starting with the important stuff.

      * An analysis from the Chemical Regulatory Consulting Board states that, "Boric acid [Borax] is only poisonous if taken internally or inhaled in large quantities." You would need to consume around a full cup of Borax for toxicity, and 1/8 tsp is generally enough per day for the entirety of the ailment.

Arthritis. Any joint pain and inflammation can be lessoned and/or cured by simply adding a pinch of Borax to a warm or hot drink any time of the day, once per day.

Bone strengthening. Because we are lacking in all minerals, and boron works in conjunction with calcium, a pinch of Borax will gradually strengthen your bones.

Brittle Bone Disease. See above.

Osteoporosis. See above.

Joints. This speaks to inflammation, and will be noticed slowly over time.

Balances hormones. Boron, and Borax is an easy way to get it, is a necessary element in our bodies. We have over 20 different hormones in our very complex bodies, and a pinch of Borax per day helps to balance them.

Menstrual cramping. See above.

Neutron absorber. Borax helps remove toxins and balance a myriad of problems.

Anti-fungal medication. Kills candida fungus – used on nail fungus, and can kill more drug-resistant forms of candida glabrada.

Cancer treatment (as one tool of many, not alone!), specifically melanoma, breast cancer, and prostate cancer – hormone-driven cancers.

Ear drops. Effective antibiotic for the treatment of ear infections and pain relief.

Eye drops. Common ingredient in eye drops, but safe in very small doses as a home remedy in distilled water.

Yeast infections.

Vaginitis [infection].

Fungal ailments of the skin and organs.

Memory loss. This may be from the removal of infections in the body, allowing the brain to function better and/or as it should.

Retention of Vitamin D, and therefore brain function.

Estrogen booster, hormone balancer.

Weight control. As a bonus side effect of all the uses listed above, when our hormones are balanced, our bodies function the way they are intended to and will return to their healthy state, including healthy "normal" weight.

*Borax is good for you!*

*(In small doses, of course.)*

# Borax as a Cleaning Agent

Brightening of cotton – both in your washing machine and by hand for delicate cotton garments, of course.

Mold and fungus killer.

Mix Borax with soap and water to make a fabulous cleaning solution.

Cutting boards, specifically wood cutting boards.

Scouring powder. Especially on copper-bottom pans and rust, but also for showers, tubs, and tiles.

Garbage disposal drain sanitizer.

Unclogging drains. Simply mix into boiling water and allow to sit and dissolve clog.

Carpet cleaner. Sprinkle into carpets, with or without baking soda, allow to sit, and then vacuum up.

Borax is a pest deterrent, but will not kill them.

Refreshening linens and mattresses.

Deodorizer. A pinch goes a long way to removing the smell from your garbage cans.

Stainless steel stains, and porcelain stains. A paste of Borax with lemon juice work wonders.

# More Uses for Borax

Fertilizer – boric acid is a crucial nutrient for all plant life, too.

Feed fruit trees, including tomatoes.

Finishing of cotton in textile factories.

Forging metal.

Soldering metal welding.

Flame and fire retardants.

Cleaners, of course. ☐


Slime for playing. The easy recipe is:

    1 Tbsp Borax

    1 cup water (distilled)

    White glue, 8 oz. bottle (Elmer's)

    Food coloring


Prevents wilting of flowers while drying for preservation.

# *Fun Facts*

Anyone wear contacts or use eye drops? Borax is an ingredient in both.

Just a reminder – a pinch (1/8 tsp) has no flavor and dissolves instantly.

Boron is the 5$^{th}$ Element on the Periodic Table.

Boron [Boric acid and Borax] is mined in Death Valley and today there is a Visitor's Center and museum in the town of Boron, CA.

Borax is non-toxic in small doses.

Not so fun fact: Borax will not kill ticks, bed bugs, lice, spiders, beetles, flies, fleas, or moths. Sorry.

If a fish tank is dirty,
clean the tank, don't
drug the fish.

Blessings!